Peanut Glasses

Barbara E. Mauzy

Revised & Expanded 2nd Edition

4880 Lower Valley Road, Atglen, PA 19310 USA

Dedication

This book is lovingly dedicated to my Grandmother and role model, Dorothy S. Drucker. She has been the one person to cheer us on from the first moment Jim and I considered a career in antiques and collectibles. With hugs and kisses from afar, this book is for you, Mom Mom!

Library of Congress Cataloging-in-Publication Data

Mauzy, Barbara E.
Peanut butter glasses / Barbara E. Mauzy. --Rev. & expanded 2nd ed.
p. cm.
ISBN 0-7643-1477-7
1. Peanut butter glasses--Collectors and collecting--United States--Catalogs.
I. Tile.
NK5440.D75 M38 2002
748.8--dc21
2001006939

Revised price guide: 2002
Copyright © 1997 & 2002 by Barbara E. Mauzy.

Original design by "Sue"
Revised 2nd edition designed by Bonnie M. Hensley
Cover design by Bruce M. Waters
Typeset in ZapfHumnst BT

ISBN: 0-7643-1477-7
Printed in China
1 2 3 4

Published by Schiffer Publishing Ltd.
4880 Lower Valley Road
Atglen, PA 19310
Phone: (610) 593-1777; Fax: (610) 593-2002
E-mail: Schifferbk@aol.com
Please visit our web site catalog at
www.schifferbooks.com

This book may be purchased from the publisher.
Include $3.95 for shipping. Please try your bookstore first.
We are always looking for people to write books on new and related subjects. If you have an idea for a book please contact us at the above address.
You may write for a free catalog.

In Europe, Schiffer books are distributed by
Bushwood Books
6 Marksbury Avenue
Kew Gardens
Surrey TW9 4JF England
Phone: 44 (0) 20-8392-8585; Fax: 44 (0) 20-8392-9876
E-mail: Bushwd@aol.com
Free postage in the UK. Europe: air mail at cost.

Contents

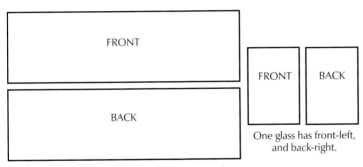

FRONT

BACK

FRONT   BACK

One glass has front-left, and back-right.

Two or more glasses have the front above and bottom below.

About the prices

This book is designed to be a tool and hopefully one that collectors and dealers alike will find useful and fun. Values vary immensely according to the condition of the glass and graphics. "Sick" glass or faded decorations are of minimal value, yet a collector may be temporarily satisfied to have a sick tumbler until a perfect one becomes available. The values assigned are for tumblers in mint condition and reflect what one could realistically expect to pay in the market place. Auctions are another story as there is no predicting how two enthusiastic collectors might bid if presented with a needed tumbler.

Neither the author nor the publisher are responsible for any outcomes resulting from consulting this book.

Acknowledgements

Without the generous sharing of the following collectors this book would not be possible as it is their tumblers that are pictured:

David G. Baker
Joan and Bob Baum
Linda S. Brown
Blaine and Judy Holland
Marge and Dennis Lerew
Ruth E. Martin
Joyce and Lynn Morgan
Timothy and Sylvia Stine
Faye and Daniel Wolfgang

…and several others who have asked to be anonymous. Thanks to you who have enjoyed using the first edition of *Peanut Butter Glasses*. It is for all of you that I have written this updated price guide.

Introduction

The first edition of *Peanut Butter Glasses* was published in 1997. It seems quite unbelievable that in such a brief period of time so much has changed and yet so much has stayed the same.

The biggest change has been in the values of peanut butter glasses. An interesting phenomenon occurred after the publication of *Peanut Butter Glasses*. People saw the book, looked at the vast.assortment of tumblers that were made, and began to search in earnest to own them all. Basic economics resulted; a huge increase in demand and a diminishing supply resulted in prices that have drastically increased. Rare now means $100 or more and the most common of glasses becomes a bargain at $5. I have received report after report of peanut butter glasses being sold at auction with the high bidder taking choice resulting in common Tulips and Poinsettias purchased for $13, $15, and even $18 each. The values assigned in this book are a fair indication of what one can expect to pay. There are bargains to be discovered and competition to overcome.

Another change is that peanut butter glasses have an ever-growing circle of enthusiasts. These colorful tumblers have been featured in several national publications as props and newspapers and periodicals devoted to collectables have also featured articles about peanut butter glasses. But most importantly, their beauty is contagious!

This brings us to what hasn't changed. Peanut butter glasses are still failing to get complete recognition. As these were geographically distributed, if you didn't grow up with these you may not know about them. Often new collectors are individuals who, after admiring a friend's collection, decide to start a collection, too. This overall lack of recognition is even reflected in eBay. There is no category for peanut butter glasses so they normally are listed with "Swanky Swigs."

Almost from the moment of publication in 1997, *Peanut Butter Glasses* became outdated as the prices dramatically rose. However, this edition has more to offer than price changes. More glasses have been found in all sizes and categories. What I cannot offer you is definitive information. For any readers new to this fun area of collecting, peanut butter glasses are tumblers that contained peanut butter sealed with a pry-off lid. One would buy the package, eat the contents, and have a tumbler for use. The colorful glassware presented in this book is primarily from the 1950s. There is virtually no existing information on the specific years of manufacture as these were unimportant product lines for glass companies of this era, and no historical information was retained. I have relied on the memories of those who grew up using them. People come to chat with Jim and me at Renninger's in Adamstown, Pennsylvania and we continue to hear conflicting information: names at the top are older; names at the bottom are older. I don't think it really matters. People buy what they like, either a style or theme, or they simply want them all! Whatever your motivation, I hope this book assists you on your hunt.

The most popular peanut butter glasses are those with flowers: Boscul Peanut Butter distributed by William Scull Company, Inc., Camden, New Jersey. The primary focus of this book is these lovely, colorful tumblers, but it is certainly worth one's time to consider the vast assortment of glassware that was used to package peanut butter.

H.B. Flowers in Lebanon, Pennsylvania produced Flower Brand Peanut Butter. Judging by the graphics on the labels these are the earliest examples presented in this book. I have found three sizes of these totally plain, clear glass tumblers: 7 ounce (3.75"), 6 ounce (3.25"), and 5 ounce (3.25").

Probably from the same time period as Flower Brand Peanut Butter, High Boy Brand Peanut Butter was marketed in this glass pail. Produced by Williams Candy Company in Chicago, this is actually the Depression Glass pattern "Block Optic." Hocking Glass Company manufactured this pattern from 1929-1933. This 6" tall, 4.75" wide pail was designed to be used as an ice bucket once emptied.

Plee-zing Peanut Butter was available in this clear goblet. This 9.5-ounce container was packed by Old Reliable Peanut Company, Inc., Suffolk, Virginia.

Flowers Peanut Butter was later available in a maple leaf tumbler. This glass was shown and listed in *Peanut Butter Glasses* as an unnamed tumbler meaning the name of the flower, or in this case tree, was not included in the graphic. Peanut butter glass collectors do seek this maple leaf tumbler, which is worth about $25.

Stylized deer in a Deco design prance around tumblers containing Blue Plate "Creamy Blend" Peanut Butter from Blue Plate Foods, Inc., New Orleans and Atlanta. They are 5.25" tall and hold twelve ounces. Looking more recent is the 5-1/8" cowboy tumbler done in yellow, blue, and red.

Peanut butter glasses were used throughout the United States and even into Canada. Other companies participating in

this marketing technique include: Luncheon Brand Churned Peanut Butter (5.5 ounces, 3.5" tall), Veteran Brand Peanut Butter (9 ounces, 4" tall) with a bubble texture found inside the glass, Verhampshire Brand Pure Peanut Butter from C.M. Tice & Co., Boston (4 ounces, 4.5" tall), and Squirrel Peanut Butter from Canada Nut Company Limited Vancouver, Canada (10 ounces, 6" tall).

Also from Canada are these 4.75" tall York tumblers that feature writing in both English and French. All feature the motto in English, 'YORK-"the one with the peanut on top"' and in French, "YORK- le seoul avec l'arachide." The elephant, monkey, and

raccoon are the only animals found so far. Probably the newest peanut butter glasses in this book are these York "Smoothy" tumblers. Found in Canada, the lids have bar codes. The denim design wraps around each 4.75" tumbler.

Swift's Peanut Butter was available in this blue "Wizard of Oz" glass. This tumbler is a "cross-collectible" meaning collectors of peanut butter glasses

and of Wizard of Oz memorabilia are interested in this item. Greater discussion of these tumblers can be found in Chapter 7. Swift also made a series of four Peanut Butter glass representing the suits of playing cards. Pictured are the heart and club tumblers which are exactly 5" tall and contained 11 oz. of product.

Proctor & Gamble, Cincinnati, Ohio, marketed Big Top Peanut Butter in a variety of glassware. The milk glass tumbler with a stylized blue trim is 5.25" tall and holds 10 ounces of product. This is one of only two peanut butter glass styles found (so far) that are not transparent glass. The "Big Top Parade" is another glass that held Big Top Peanut Butter. The 5" tall tumbler features clowns, balloons, a bass drum, and confetti in red, white, and blue. Big Top Peanut Butter was also available in pressed glass containers including a sherbet,

which is shown, and a tumbler in clear glass and in milk glass (5.5" tall, 3" diameter). Cups and saucers were also made in this pressed glass style. I

have been told that matching plates were also manufactured, but I have not seen one. This design is sometimes referred to as the "Peanut Butter Pattern" of glassware. Pieces sell for about $5 each. The final example of Big Top Peanut Butter is the tumbler with gold and pink polka dots.

Derby's Peter Pan Peanut Butter from Chicago was also sold in clear tumblers. The glass on the left is about 5" tall and holds 12 ounces. The tumbler on the right is 4.75" tall and holds 9.5 ounces. Both tumblers have a beaded rim at the top.

Sweet Clover Brand Homogenized Peanut Butter was available in a Cocker Spaniel tumbler. One would presume that other dog tumblers with the white name at the top also contained Sweet Clover Brand.

Two sides of the Cream Dove Homogenized Peanut Butter glass (below) are labeled for measurements in ounces and tablespoons (shown) as well as cups and pints. This 5″ tall glass was made by Hazel-Atlas.

The primary focus of this book is Boscul Peanut Butter as this is the brand packaged in the lovely flowered tumblers. If you are fortunate enough to find an unopened container of Boscul Peanut butter expect to pay well over $150. This is a seller's market as these are not being found anymore. The people to whom I have spoken who possess an unopened peanut butter glass would never even consider selling such a prized and coveted treasure.

There are three main sizes of Boscul peanut butter glasses: iced tea, standard, and juice. Standard tumblers are found with the name at the top and the name at the bottom and have different measurements as shown below. Juice tumblers are also found with the names at the bottom and top, but are the same size. Here are some numbers:

	Height	Diameter	Ounces
Iced tea	6 ¼″	2 14/16″	14
Standard-name at top	5″	2 12/16″	11
Standard-name at bottom	5″	2 11/16″	10
Juice	3 ¾″	2 3/16″	5

To determine capacity, water was placed to the very rim of the tumbler.

Three examples with names at the top:

Asters   **Dogwood**   **Violet**

Four examples with names at the bottom:

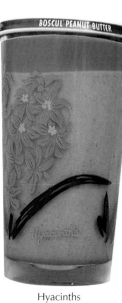

Canterbury Bell

Fawnlily

Black-Eyed Susan

Hyacinths

The lid on the lower left still maintains the original price of 39 cents. I have seen one lid with a 29 cent price. Much of what is known about these glasses is based on memories. One story shared with me is that Boscul Peanut Butter was 39 cents with the reusable tumbler or 37 cents in a disposable container. So if the woman of the house chose to afford the additional 2 cents there were flowered glasses in that kitchen.

Three views of a Boscul Coffee can advertizing "Creamy-smooth Boscul Peanut Butter... in glasses decorated with gay flower designs constantly changing."

Two views of the "125th ANNIVERSARY OF QUALITY" Boscul Coffee can. This advertisement for their glasses is a different graphic than the other can.

The Three Sizes of Glasses

The ultimate collection will involve every combination of name, color, and size available. People often proudly display threesomes of tea, standard, and juice size peanut butter glasses together in a prominent fashion. A few samples of these possibilities are shown here.

The following flower designs can be found in all three sizes. Happy hunting!

Red Amaryllis
Blue Columbine
Purple Michaelmas Daisy
Blue Morning Glory
White Sweet Scented Gladiolus
Red Tulips

☐ **Amaryllis** Tea, Standard, Juice

☐ **Columbine** Tea, Standard, Juice

☐ **Michaelmas Daisy** Juice, Standard, Tea

☐ **Michaelmas Daisy**

☐ **Sweet Scented Gladiolus** Tea, Standard, Juice

Chapter 1

FLOWERS Standard Size, Names at Top

There are 84 different glasses in 35 different names. These tumblers hold one more ounce of liquid and are 1/16″ wider than the standard glasses with the name at the bottom.

The most popular tumblers are usually those that are the most difficult to locate. These include: bluish-purple Pansy with pale yellow, red Morning-Glory, and gold and orange Zinnias. The Poinsettias continue to be plentiful and are often collected for use at Christmas.

Collecting patterns still remain the same since my comments in 1997. Some people collect either the name at the top or the name at the bottom, with the name at the top being more popular. There are far fewer combinations in this design making the process of building a collection quite manageable.

☐ **Asters** blue name - light blue flowers with dark blue centers and a few dark blue lines coming out from centers (reverse coloration of fourth Asters) $12

☐ **Asters** blue name - light blue bushy flowers having each petal outlined in dark blue also with a dark blue line in the center of each petal $12

☐ **Asters** blue name - dark blue bushy flowers with small amounts of light blue $12

☐ **Asters** blue name - dark blue flowers with light blue centers and a few light blue lines coming out from centers (reverse coloration of first Asters) $12

☐ **Carnation** red name - red flowers with white lines throughout (reverse coloration of second Carnation) $10

☐ **Azalea** black name - red flowers with black centers and some black lines along edges of petals $10

☐ **Camellia** red name - red flowers with darker highlights $10

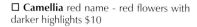

☐ **Carnation** red name - white flowers with red lines throughout (reverse coloration of first Carnation) $10

☐ **Carnation** red name - red flowers with darker red highlights $10

☐ **Christmas Rose** white name - white flowers with gold centers $10

☐ **Chrysanthemum** rust color name at top – gold flowers with rust highlights very light green leaves $15

☐ **Chrysanthemum** goldish yellow name at top – white flowers with goldish highlights dark green leaves $12

☐ **Chrysanthemum** gold name at top – white flowers with gold highlights extremely dark green leaves $12

☐ **Chrysanthemum** orange name - gold flowers with orange lines in each petal $12

☐ **Cornflower** white name – blue flowers with white centers $18

☐ **Cornflower** small blue name near top – blue flowers with white centers $18

☐ **Chrysanthemum** yellow name - white flowers with yellow lines in each petal $12

19

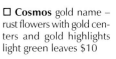

☐ **Cosmos** gold name – rust flowers with gold centers and gold highlights light green leaves $10

☐ **Cosmos** gold name – rust flowers with gold centers and gold highlights dark green leaves $10

☐ **Cornflower** blue name - light blue flowers with darker blue centers and random lines $18

☐ **Daffodil** orange-gold name - gold flowers with orange highlights $12

☐ **Cosmos** gold name - rust flowers with gold centers and a few gold lines coming out from centers (reverse coloration of other Cosmos) $10

☐ **Daffodil** gold name - white flowers with gold highlights $10

☐ **Daffodil** yellow gold name at top – white flowers with yellow gold highlights light green leaves $18

☐ **Cosmos** rust name - gold flowers with rust centers and a few rust lines coming out from centers (reverse coloration of other Cosmos) $10

20

☐ **Dahlia** blue name - light blue flowers with dark blue highlights in top half of blossoms $12

☐ **Dahlia** black name - red flowers with black highlights $12

☐ **Dahlia** black name (letters of name are thinner) - coral-red flowers with black highlights $12

☐ **Dahlia** black name in empty space between flowers – coral-red flowers with black highlights $15

☐ **Daisy** black name - yellow flowers with black centers and black lines mainly in top half of blossoms $10

☐ **Daisy** red-orange name - gold flowers with red-orange centers and highlights $10

☐ **Day-Lily** gold name - gold flowers with orange centers and lines $14

☐ **Daisy** black name - brownish-gold flowers with black centers and black lines mainly in top half of blossoms $10

☐ **Daisy** black name - yellow flowers with black center and black lines mainly in top half of blossoms $10

☐ **Day-Lily** yellow name - yellow flowers with orange centers and lines $14

☐ **Dogwood** yellow name - white flowers with yellow dots in centers $14

☐ **Dogwood** yellow name - pink flowers with gold dots in centers $16

☐ **"GIANT" Zinnias** red name - white bushy flowers with red separating each petal and acting as dominant color $20

☐ **Easter Lily** gold name - white flowers with gold centers $14

☐ **"GIANT" Zinnias** orange name - orange bushy flowers with darker orange separating each petal $18

☐ **Gloxinina** white name - maroon flowers with white centers, edges, and lines $14

☐ **Gloxinina** white name - blue flowers with white centers, edges, and lines $16

☐ **Hibiscus** white name - white flowers with pink centers and highlights $14

☐ **Hybrid Tea Rose** mustard name – yellow flowers with mustard highlights and leaves that are lighter than the other yellow Hybrid Tea Rose $18

☐ **Hybrid Tea Rose** mustard name - gold flowers with mustard highlights on each petal $14

☐ **Iris** yellow name - gray flowers with yellow highlights $20

☐ **Iris** blue name - blue flowers with darker blue highlights $16

☐ **Hybrid Tea Rose** red name - red flowers with darker red highlights on each petal $10

☐ **Laurel** red name - white flowers with red edges $10
☐ **Marigold** burnt orange name - burnt orange and gold flowers $15
☐ **Morning-Glory** white name - red flowers with white centers and highlights $20
☐ **Morning-Glory** white name - blue flowers with white centers and highlights $15

☐ **Nasturtium** black name - red flowers with black centers and lines coming out from centers $10

☐ **Nasturtium** brownish-orange name - orange flowers with darker orange centers and lines coming out from centers $14

☐ **Orchid (not pictured)** small bluish gray name on angle at top – bluish gray flowers with blue highlights and light green leaves $25

☐ **Orchid (not pictured)** small gray name on angle at top – gray flowers with yellow highlights $25

☐ **Pansy** black name - yellow and black flowers $10

☐ **Pansy** pale yellow name - bluish-purple and pale yellow flowers $28

☐ **Petunia** white name - blue flowers with white highlights $18

☐ **Petunia** white name - pink flowers with white highlights $16

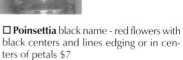

☐ **Poinsettia** black name - red flowers with black centers and lines edging or in centers of petals $7

☐ **Poinsettia** orange name - red flowers with orange centers $7

☐ **Rhododendron** red name - pinkish-coral flowers with red highlights $18

☐ **Poppy** red name - red flowers with black centers and several lines coming out from centers $10

☐ **Rhododendron** black name - red flowers with black highlights $10

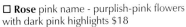

☐ **Rose** pink name - purplish-pink flowers with dark pink highlights $18

☐ **Rose** pink name - pink flowers with darker pink highlights $18

☐ **Rose** red name - yellow flowers with red highlights $14

☐ **Rose** pink name - white flowers with pink highlights $18

☐ **Rose** red name - red flowers with darker red highlights $10

☐ **Rose** dark red name – dark red flowers with extremely dark red highlights $14

☐ **Rose** dark red name – red flowers with dark red highlights $14

☐ **Sunflower** yellow name - yellow flowers with black centers and highlights $14

☐ **Tulips** red name - red flowers with darker red highlights $8

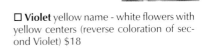

☐ **Violet** yellow name - white flowers with yellow centers (reverse coloration of second Violet) $18

☐ **Sunflower** gold name - gold flowers with black centers and highlights $14

☐ **Violet** white name - yellow flowers with white centers (reverse coloration of first Violet) $25

☐ **Violet** yellow name - purple flowers with yellow centers $20

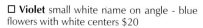

☐ **Violet** small white name on angle - blue flowers with white centers $20

☐ **Violet** white name - blue flowers with white centers $20

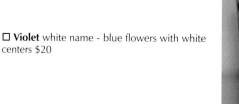

☐ **Windflower** blue name - pale yellow centers with white lines coming out from centers $18

☐ **Zinnia** orange name - gold bushy flowers with orange separating each petal $20

☐ **Windflower** white name – white flowers with pink centers $18

☐ **Zinnias** orange name - gold and orange flowers with pure gold bud near bottom $20

31

Chapter 2

FLOWERS Standard Size, Names at Bottom

There are 367 different glasses with 103 different names of flowers at the bottom of the glasses in this narrower standard size. This represents an addition of 36 tumblers since the first book was published. There is a huge array of variations and I have attempted to show and explain them all. The differences may be as minute as a dot under a name or the shade of green in the leaves.

Some of the tumblers in this chapter are quite rare. If two collectors needing the same tumbler should happen to compete against one another in an auction situation there is no telling what price would result. The values assigned should also help to indicate the rarity of the given tumbler as more elusive tumblers simply have a higher value.

Collecting patterns are as diverse as collectors themselves. We have met focused collectors who collect only wild flowers, iris growers who collect irises, people looking for the flowers that are planted in their gardens, and so on. The vast majority of collectors are trying to find all of the tumblers made. To you all, good luck. Jim and I have yet to own the "Tea Seed!"

☐ **African Violet** blue name near center - blue flowers with gold centers $20

☐ **African Violet** pale blue name near center - pale blue flowers with orange centers $20

□ **African Violet** blue name at very bottom - entirely blue flowers with leaves all over not just at bottom $30

□ **African Violet** pink name near center - pink flowers with yellow centers $30

□ **African Violet** mauve name near center - mauve flowers with gold centers $30

□ **African Violet** purple name near center - purple flowers with gold centers $30

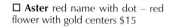

☐ **Amaryllis** red name - red flowers with white centers and lines coming out from centers $18

☐ **Aster** red name - red flowers with gold centers $15

☐ **Aster** red name with dot – red flower with gold centers $15

☐ **Amaryllis** red name - red flowers with pale pink centers and white lines coming out from centers $20

☐ **American Lotus** gold name - gold flowers with mustard centers $14

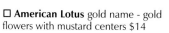

☐ **Aster** light blue name near middle – light blue flowers with dark blue centers and some dark blue highlights $20

☐ **Aster** blue name - blue flowers with gold centers $12

☐ **Aster** white name - white flowers with gold centers $14

☐ **Aster** pink name - pink flowers with gold centers $18

☐ **Aster** blue name - light blue bushy flowers having each petal outlined in dark blue also with a dark blue line in the center of each petal $14

☐ **Asters** blue name - light blue bushy flowers having each petal outlined in dark blue also with a dark blue line in the center of each petal $12
☐ **Asters (not pictured)** blue name near middle that crosses through stem – blue flowers with dark blue highlights $20
☐ **Azalea** white name - white flowers with pink centers and highlights $14
☐ **Azalea** red name - red flowers with black centers and highlights $10
☐ **Bellflower** blue name - blue flowers with orange centers $12

☐ **Bittersweet** orange name - orange and gold berries $25

☐ **Bittersweet** red name - red and gold berries $25

☐ **Black-eyed Susan** yellow name - yellow flowers with black centers $30

☐ **Blue Beauty Water Lily** aqua name - aqua flowers with yellow centers $25

☐ **Blue Beauty Water Lily** blue name - blue flowers with yellow centers $25

☐ **Black-eyed Susan** gold name - gold flowers with black centers $30

☐ **Blue Beauty Water Lily** aqua name – aqua flowers with no center coloration $25

☐ **Calendula** yellow name - entirely yellow flowers $14

☐ **California Poppy** yellow name - yellow flowers with green centers $12

☐ **Calla Lily** white name - white flowers with yellow centers and bases $20

☐ **California Poppy** yellow name with dot – yellow flowers with green centers $12

☐ **Calla Lily** white name with dot under name – white flowers with yellow centers and bases $20

☐ **Camellia** red name - red flowers with darker red highlights $10

☐ **Canterbury Bell** white name - white flowers with gold centers $12

☐ **Camellia** red name with dot – red flower with dark red highlights and medium green leaves $10

☐ **Canterbury Bell** white name – white flowers with yellow centers & medium green leaves $12

☐ **Canterbury Bell** blue name - blue flowers with orange centers $18

☐ **Cardinal Climber** red name - red flowers with pinkish-white highlights $25

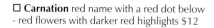

☐ **Cardinal Climber** orange name - orange flowers with gold highlights $25

☐ **Carnation** red name with a red dot below - red flowers with darker red highlights $12

☐ **Carnation** white name - white flowers with red highlights $14

☐ **Carnation** red name with red dot just above dark leaves – dark red flowers with darker red highlights $12

☐ **Carnation** red name in empty area above light green leaves – red flowers with some dark red highlights $12

☐ **Carnation** red name above dark green leaves – red flowers with dark red highlights and red buds with red stems $12

40

☐ **Christmas Rose** white name - white flowers with gold centers $12

☐ **Chrysanthemum** green name - entirely yellow flowers $14

☐ **Christmas Rose** white name in middle going straight across – white flowers with orange centers medium green leaves $12

☐ **Chrysanthemum** red name - red flowers with yellow centers $14

☐ **Chrysanthemum** green name - entirely white flowers $18

☐ **Chrysanthemum** red name - red flowers with pale yellow centers $14

41

☐ **Chrysanthemum** green name at bottom between flowers – solid yellow flowers dark green leaves $14

☐ **Clematis** blue name - blue flowers with yellow centers $14

☐ **Columbine** light turquoise blue name - light turquoise blue flowers with white centers $12

☐ **Clematis** maroon name - maroon flowers with yellow centers $18

☐ **Columbine** white name - white flowers with yellow centers $20

☐ **Columbine** red name - red flowers with white centers $20

☐ **Columbine** red name - red flowers with yellow centers $12

☐ **Columbine** pale blue name - pale blue flowers with white centers $12

☐ **Columbine** blue name almost totally horizontal - blue flowers with white centers $12

☐ **Columbine** yellow name almost totally horizontal - yellow flowers with white centers $20

☐ **Columbine** green name - multiple shades of blue flowers with gold centers and leaves of dark and light green $30

☐ **Columbine** yellow name at bottom – yellow flowers with white centers dark green leaves $20

☐ **Columbine** blue name at bottom – blue flowers with white center dark green leaves $12

☐ **Columbine** blue name at bottom with dot - blue flowers with white center dark green leaves $12

☐ **Columbine** green name - pink flowers with gold centers and leaves of dark and light green $30

☐ **Cornflower** blue name near middle - blue and white flowers with white centers $18

☐ **Cornflower** green name - blue and white flowers with white centers $18

☐ **Columbine** maroon name – maroon flowers with yellow centers $22

☐ **Columbine** (not shown) maroon name – maroon flowers with white centers $25

☐ **Cornflower** blue name near middle – blue flowers with white centers $18

☐ **Cosmos** gold name - gold flowers with red centers and red highlights $14

☐ **Cosmos** orange name - orange flowers with yellow centers and yellow highlights $25

☐ **Cosmos** coral name - coral flowers with yellow centers $25

☐ **Cosmos** rust name - rust flowers with gold centers and gold highlights $25

☐ **Cosmos** burgundy name with a burgundy dot below - burgundy flowers with gold centers and lines coming out from centers $14

☐ **Cosmos** pink name – pink flowers with yellow and pink dots in the centers $18

☐ **Cosmos** gold name near center - white flowers with gold centers and gold highlights and leaves both green and white $12

☐ **Cosmos** yellow name (no dot) near middle – yellow flowers with maroon centers and thicker maroon highlights $14
☐ **Cosmos** yellow name near middle – yellow flowers with orange centers and orange highlights and darker green leaves $14
☐ **Cosmos** yellow name with dot near middle – yellow flowers with maroon centers and maroon highlights $14

☐ **Cosmos** gold name - gold flowers with orange centers $14

☐ **Crocus** yellow name - yellow flowers with purple dots in centers and purple flowers with white dots in centers $30

☐ **Cosmos** burgundy name (no dot) – burgundy flowers with gold centers and lines coming out from centers $14

☐ **Cosmos** orange name – orange flowers with gold centers and gold lines coming out from centers, light green leaves with some clear glass showing through $25

☐ **Daffodil** pale yellow name - three yellow flowers with golden orange highlights; one blossom points up, one straight out, and one down. RARE $30

☐ **Crimson cactus** white name - red flowers with white centers and white stars in between blossoms $40

47

☐ **Daffodil** yellow name - entirely yellow flowers $14

☐ **Daffodil** white name - white flowers with yellow highlights $14

☐ **Daffodil** yellow name with a yellow dot below - yellow flowers with darker yellow centers $14

☐ **Daffodil** white name - white flowers with pink center and light green leaves $20

☐ **Daffodil** yellow name at bottom – yellow flowers with orange center lighter green leaves $25

☐ **Daffodil** green name at bottom – gold flowers with orange highlights dark green leaves $25

☐ **Daffodil** gold name at bottom – gold flowers with orange highlights light green leaves $25

☐ **Daffodil** white name - white flowers with pink centers and dark green leaves $5-8

☐ **Daffodil** yellow name - yellow flowers with orange centers $18

49

☐ **Daffodils** white name - white flowers with yellow highlights $18

☐ **Daffodils** yellow name with dot above leaves – solid yellow flowers dark green leaves $25

☐ **Daffodils** yellow name - entirely yellow flowers $14

☐ **Dahlia** red name - red flowers $18

☐ **Daffodils** yellow name - yellow flowers with orange highlights $3-5

□ **Dahlia** pink name - pink flowers with white highlights $25

□ **Dahlia autumn** red name - small red flowers with white edges and lines with no green leaves $10

□ **Dahlia** red name - red flowers with black highlights $12

□ **Daisy** gold name under drooping blossom – gold flowers with red center and red highlights and yellow stems $18

□ **Dahlia autumn** yellow name - small yellow flowers with gold edges and lines with no green leaves $18

□ **Dogwood** white name - white flowers with gold dots in centers $14

□ **Daisy** gold name - gold flowers with red centers and highlights $14

□ **Dianthus Pink** red name - white flowers with red centers and entirely red flowers $8

□ **Dogwood** green name - white flowers on top half and pink flowers on bottom half with green circles in centers $40

□ **Dogwood** pink name in middle that crosses stem – pink flowers with gold dots in centers $14

□ **Dogwood** pink name just above leaves – pink flowers with gold dots in centers $14

☐ **Dwarf Iris** light blue name - light blue flowers with gold centers $30

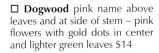

☐ **Dogwood** pink name above leaves and at side of stem – pink flowers with gold dots in center and lighter green leaves $14

☐ **Dogwood** pink name with dot above leaves and at side of stem – pink flowers with gold dots in center and darker green leaves $14

☐ **Easter Lily** white name - large white flowers with gold centers and darker green leaves spreading horizontally along bottom $18

☐ **Easter Lily** white name near center - large white flowers with gold centers and lighter green leaves spreading horizontally along bottom $18

☐ **Dogwood** white name with "D" printed rather than script – white flowers with gold dots in center $14

☐ **Easter Lily** white name - small white flowers with orange centers on vertical darker green stems $18

☐ **Dwarf Iris** navy blue name - navy blue flowers with orange centers $30

53

☐ **Fairyland orchid cactus** green name - pink flowers with green centers $30

☐ **Easter Lily** white name - small white flowers with less prominent orange centers on vertical darker green stems $18

☐ **Fawn Lily** pink name - yellow flowers on stems that are pink at their bases $30

☐ **Easter Lily** white name in between leaves - large white flowers with gold centers and darker green leaves spreading horizontally along bottom $18

☐ **Fiesta Cosmos** yellow name - yellow flowers with black dots in centers $20

☐ **Fiesta Cosmos** gold name - gold flowers with black dots in centers $20

☐ **Eastern White Pine** brown name - brown pine cones with green needles $20

☐ **Gentian** green name - multi-colored blue flowers with dark and light green leaves $35

☐ **Gentian (not pictured)** green name – light blue and very light blue flowers with dark and light green leaves $25

☐ **Giant Velvet Flower** red name - flowers blend gold, red, pale olive green, and dark olive green $30

☐ **Fiesta Cosmos** yellow name – yellow flowers with black and yellow dots in the centers, no stems or leaves $20

☐ **Fiesta Cosmos** bright yellow name – bright yellow flowers with black and yellow dots in the centers and light green leaves $20

☐ **Giant Velvet Flower** red name - gold flowers with red highlights $30

☐ **Forget-Me-Not** blue name - blue flowers with yellow centers $20

☐ **Forget-Me-Not** turquoise name – turquoise flowers with pale yellow centers and light green leaves $20

☐ **Giant Velvet Flower** blue name - gold flowers with blue highlights, blue flowers with gold highlights, and blue flowers with white highlights $25

☐ **Giant Velvet Flower** blue name - flowers blend gold, blue, pale olive green, and dark olive green $30

☐ **Gloxinia** white name - blue flowers with white centers, edges, and lines $18

☐ **Gloxinia** white name - red flowers with white centers, edges, and lines $18

☐ **Gloxinia** white name - navy blue flowers with white centers, edges, and lines $18

☐ **Gloxinia** white name near middle – light blue flowers with white edges and lighter green leaves $18

☐ **Gloxinia** white name with dot near middle – medium blue flowers with white edges and medium green leaves $18

☐ **Gloxinia** white name near middle – maroon flowers with white edges and dark green leaves $18

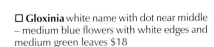

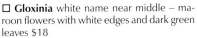

☐ **Holly** red name at very bottom - small clusters of berries that may have green or white detailing among two branches of leaves wrapped horizontally around glass $10

☐ **Gloxinia** white name near middle with dot (name is 1" long) – burgundy flowers with white edges and white highlights and light green leaves $18

☐ **Gloxinia** white name near middle (name is 1.25" long) – burgundy flowers with thinner white edges and barely visible white highlights and dark green leaves $18

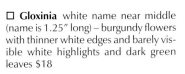

☐ **Holly** red name up from bottom - berries are completely red on one branch of leaves wrapped diagonally around glass $10

☐ **Holly (not pictured)** green name - vertical branches of leaves with berries $10

57

□ **Hyacinth** green name - blue flowers with yellow centers $18

□ **Holly** red name – branch raps horizontally around tumbler ending with four berries $10

□ **Holly** red name – branch raps horizontally around tumbler ending with seven berries $10

□ **Holly** red name on slight angle - branch raps horizontally around tumbler ending with four berries $10

□ **Hyacinth** yellow name - yellow flowers with red centers $18

□ **Holly Leaves** green name - vertical branches of leaves with berries $10

□ **Hyacinth** white name - white flowers with yellow centers $14

□ **Hyacinth** green name - purple flowers with yellow centers $20

□ **Hyacinth** pink name - pink flowers with red centers $14

☐ **Hyacinth** blue name - dark and light blue flowers $30

☐ **Hyacinths** white name - white flowers with yellow centers $14

☐ **Hyacinth** blue name – blue flowers with golden orange centers $18

☐ **Hyacinths** pink name at bottom – pink flowers with maroon centers $18

☐ **Hyacinths** yellow name at bottom – yellow flowers with maroon centers $18

☐ **Hyacinths** blue name - blue flowers with yellow centers $18

☐ **Hybrid Tea Rose** green name - orange flowers with red highlights $18

☐ **Hybrid Tea Rose** green name - red flowers with darker red highlights $12

☐ **Hybrid Tea Rose** green name - gold flowers with golden orange highlights $14

☐ **Hybrid Tea Rose** green name - deep red flowers with even deeper red highlights and darker green leaves than previous glass $12

☐ **Hybrid Tea Rose** green name - yellow and pale yellow flowers $14

☐ **Hybrid Tea Rose** green name - yellow flowers with gold highlights $14

☐ **Hybrid Tea Rose** large Kelly green name – yellow flowers with white highlights $14

☐ **Iris** yellow name - gray flowers with yellow highlights $14

☐ **Hybrid Tea Rose** green name - pink flowers with darker pink highlights $18

☐ **Hybrid Tea Rose** green name - white flowers with pink highlights $18

☐ **Iris** gray name - gray flowers with purple highlights $18

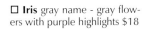

☐ **Iris** gray name - gray flowers with yellow highlights $14

☐ **Japanese Lily** yellow name - yellow flowers with red centers $25

☐ **Iris** blue name - blue flowers with darker blue highlights $14

☐ **Jonquil** yellow name with a yellow dot below - yellow flowers with pale yellow centers on some $18

☐ **Iris** gray name with dot – gray flowers with purple highlights $18

□ **Jonquil** yellow name - yellow flowers with pale yellow centers on some $18

□ **Laurel** white name - white flowers with red edges $10

□ **Laurel** pink name - pink flowers with red edges $12

☐ **Lenten Rose** pink name - pink flowers with yellow centers $14

☐ **Lilac** green name - raspberry flowers with gold centers $14

☐ **Lenten Rose** white name - white flowers with yellow centers $10

☐ **Lilac** green name - white flowers with gold centers $14

☐ **Lilac** green name - pink flowers with maroon centers $18

☐ **Lilac** green name - purple flowers with gold centers $18

☐ **Lilac (not pictured)** green name – white flowers with gold centers $14

☐ **Lily of the Valley** white name - white flowers $18

☐ **Magnolia** white name - white flowers with yellow centers $12

☐ **Marigold** burnt orange name - burnt orange and gold flowers $14

☐ **Marliac Rose Water Lily** coral name - coral flowers with yellow centers $18

☐ **Mexican Sunflower** orange name near bottom on angle – orange flowers with yellow centers and some yellow highlights and dark green leaves $20

☐ **Mexican Sunflower** orange name at very bottom – orange flowers with yellow centers with lots of plain glass showing and very dark green leaves $20

☐ **Mexican Sunflower** red name at bottom - red flowers with gold centers $20

☐ **Michaelmas Daisy** purple name at bottom - purple flowers with gold centers $20

☐ **Michaelmas Daisy** blue name - blue flowers with gold centers and very narrow unpainted lines through centers of petals $18

☐ **Michaelmas Daisy** blue name - blue flowers with yellow centers and more pronounced unpainted lines through centers of petals $18

□ **Morning Glory** red name near middle on angle – red flowers with white highlights and very dark green leaves $25

□ **Morning-Glory** red name near middle with hyphen – red flowers with white highlights and lighter green leaves $25

□ **Mistletoe** white name up from bottom - three branches with white berries that have dots $16

□ **Mistletoe** white name at bottom - two branches with solid white berries $20

□ **Morning Glory** blue name with dot above dark green leaves – blue flower with white highlights $25

□ **Morning Glory (not pictured)** blue name near middle on angle "G" looks similar to "J" – large blue flowers with white highlights and medium green leaves $25

□ **Mockorange** white name - white flowers with yellow centers $14

□ **Morning Glory (not pictured)** blue name near middle on angle – smaller blue flowers with white highlights and smaller medium green leaves $25

☐ **Morning-Glory** blue name near middle - blue flowers with white highlights $16

☐ **Morning-Glory** pale blue name at top in small script - pale blue flowers with white highlights $20

☐ **Mrs.J.H.Pring Water Lily** white name - white flowers with yellow centers $20

☐ **Narcissus** yellow name - yellow flowers with red centers $14

☐ **Narcissus** white name - white flowers with red centers $12

☐ **Narcissus** white name on angle near middle – white flower with orange-gold centers and light green leaves $12

☐ **Narcissus** white name - white flowers with orange centers $10

☐ **Orchid** gray name - gray flowers with yellow highlights $20

☐ **Orchid** gray name - gray flowers with white highlights $20

☐ **Night-blooming cereus cactus** green name with "e" written like a backward "3" – white flowers with green dots near centers $20

☐ **Night-blooming cereus cactus** green name all in script – white flowers with green dots near centers $20

☐ **Orchid** gray name near middle – pink flowers with gray highlights and gray stems $20

☐ **Orchid** white name - light gray flowers with white highlights $20

☐ **Orchid** blue name near top - light blue flowers with darker blue highlights $20

☐ **Orchid** gray name - gray flowers with purple highlights $20

☐ **Orchid** gray name - gray flowers with bluish-purple highlights and darker green leaves than other Orchid with this combination $20

☐ **Orchid** white name below blossom - gray flowers with raspberry highlights $25

☐ **Orchid** white name near top - gray flowers with yellow highlights $20

☐ **Orchid** white name near middle - gray flowers with raspberry highlights $25

☐ **Orchid** pink name near top - pink flowers with darker pink highlights $25

☐ **Orchid** white name - white flowers with purple highlights $25

☐ **Oriental Poppy** coral name - coral flowers with black centers $20

☐ **Oriental Poppy** red name - red flowers with black centers $20

73

□ **Pansy** yellow name near middle – yellow with really dark brown centers with lighter green leaves $14

□ **Pansy** really dark brown name near middle – yellow flowers with really dark brown centers $14

□ **Pansy** green name - smaller pink and black flowers with dark green and light green leaves $35

□ **Pansy** green name - smaller yellow and black flowers with dark green and light green leaves $35

□ **Pansy** yellow name near middle - yellow flowers with very dark brown centers and dark green leaves $14

□ **Peony** red name - red flowers with yellow $14

Petunia red name - red flowers with pale yellow centers $14

Peony red name - red flowers with gold $14

Petunia red name - red flowers with gold centers $14

☐ **Petunia** red name - red flowers with yellow centers $14

☐ **Phlox** red name - red flowers with pink centers $18

☐ **Phlox** red name - deep red flowers and white flowers with deep red centers that blend into green at bottoms $18

☐ **Phlox** white name - red flowers with white centers $18

☐ **Phlox** red name - red flowers with white centers $18

☐ **Pin Cushion Flower** white name - white flowers with blue "pins" $20

☐ **Phlox** red name - light red flowers and white flowers with light red centers $18

☐ **Pin Cushion Flower** blue name - blue flowers with white "pins" and darker green leaves than the previous glass $18

☐ **Phlox** white name – coral flowers with white centers and white flowers with coral centers on reverse side with no green mixing into flowers and one white stem $18

☐ **Phlox** red name – red flowers with white centers and white flowers with red centers with no green mixing into flowers $18

☐ **Pine** brown name near center - branches are full of needles and smaller pine cones $18

☐ **Poinsettia** red name just above dark green leaves - red flowers with orange centers $10

☐ **Poinsettia** red name on angle - red flowers having detailed petals that show veins with orange centers $10

☐ **Pine** brown name - branches have few needles with large pine cones, white lines of snow encircle top of glass $20

☐ **Poinsettia** red name just above light green leaves that have red lines - red flowers with yellow centers $10

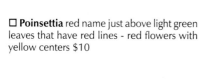

☐ **Poinsettia** red name on angle near middle - small red flowers with much clear glass exposed $12

☐ **Poinsettia** yellow name - yellow flowers with orange centers and light green leaves $20

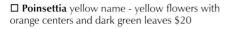

☐ **Poinsettia** yellow name - yellow flowers with orange centers and dark green leaves $20

☐ **Poinsettia** cream-colored name - cream-colored flowers with red-orange centers $20

☐ **Poinsettia** white name - white flowers with yellow centers and narrow bare veins in leaves $20

☐ **Poppy** red name below two touching blossoms - red flowers with black centers and several lines coming out from centers $10

☐ **Poinsettia** white name - white flowers with orange centers and broader bare veins in leaves $20

☐ **Poppy** red name in empty space - red flowers with black centers and several lines coming from centers $10

☐ **Poinsettia** red name above lighter green leaves – red flowers with orange centers $10

☐ **Poppy** red name with dot at very bottom – red flowers with black centers and black highlights medium green leaves $10

☐ **Poppy** red name at very bottom – red flowers with black centers and black highlights medium green leaves $10

- ☐ **Primrose** gold name on angle - smaller gold flowers with orange centers $12

- ☐ **Primrose** yellow name - larger yellow flowers with white centers $16

- ☐ **Primrose** red name on angle - smaller red flowers with yellow centers $12

- ☐ **Primrose** red name - larger red flowers with white centers $12

☐ **Primrose** blue name - larger blue flowers with white centers $18

☐ **Primrose** orange-red name - larger orange-red flowers with yellow centers $12

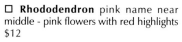

☐ **Rhododendron** pink name near middle - pink flowers with red highlights $12

☐ **Rhododendron** red name near middle - red flowers with black highlights $12

☐ **Rhododendron** coral name near middle - coral flowers with red highlights $16

☐ **Rose** white name - entirely white flowers $18

☐ **Rose** gold name - white flowers with gold centers $14

☐ **Rose** red name - entirely red flowers $14

☐ **Rose** red name near middle close to blossom - entirely red flowers $10

☐ **Rose** gold name - entirely red flowers with partially opened blossom above name $12

☐ **Rose** red name near middle just above leaves - entirely red flowers $10

☐ **Rose** green name - pink flowers with red highlights $18

☐ **Rose** yellow flowers with red highlights $14

☐ **Rose** white name - white flowers with paler pink highlights and lighter green leaves $18

☐ **Rose** gold name - entirely gold flowers $18

☐ **Rose** gold name - yellow flowers with gold centers $18

☐ **Rose** white name - white flowers with darker pink highlights and less white exposed $18

☐ **Rose** white name - white flowers with paler pink highlights and darker green leaves $18

☐ **Rose** yellow name - blue flowers with yellow centers $16

☐ **Rose** green name near middle – red flowers with dark red highlights, green leaves with light green veins $12

☐ **Rose** red name near middle with dot underneath – red flowers with dark red highlights $12

☐ **Rose** red name near middle – red flowers with dark red highlights $10

☐ **Rose** red name near middle – extremely dark flower with extremely dark red highlights very dark green leaves $10

☐ **Rose** red name near very bottom among leaves – red flowers with dark red highlights $10

☐ **Rose** red name with dot near very bottom among leaves – bright red flowers with red highlights $10

☐ **Rose** white name with dot – white flowers with pink highlights $18

☐ **St. Louis Water Lily** gold name - gold flowers with yellow centers $30

☐ **Scabiosa** white name - white flowers with blue "pins" $20

☐ **Scabiosa** gray name - gray flowers with white "pins" $20

☐ **Scabiosa** white name - white flower with red "pins" $20

☐ **Spring Crocus** green name - white flowers with gold centers $16

☐ **Shasta Daisy** white name on slight angle written in script except for a printed "s" – white flowers with gold centers and darker green leaves $18

☐ **Shasta Daisy** white name on a stronger angle written totally in script – white flower with gold centers and lighter green leaves $18

☐ **Spring Crocus** purple name - purple flowers with gold centers $20

☐ **Snowberry** white name - white berries with dark green leaves $30

☐ **Snowberry (not pictured)** – white name on angle – white berries with dark green leaves $30

87

☐ **Spring Crocus** blue name with a blue dot below - blue flowers with gold centers $20

☐ **Spring Crocus** blue name - blue flowers with gold centers $16

☐ **Spring Crocus** green name - blue flowers with orange centers $20

☐ **Spring Crocus** raspberry name - raspberry flowers with gold centers $20

☐ **Spring Crocus** yellow name - yellow flowers with blue centers $25

☐ **Spring Crocus** green name - purple flowers with gold centers $20

☐ **Spring Crocus** white name – white flowers with gold centers $20

☐ **Spring Crocus** blue name on angle – blue flowers with gold centers $20

☐ **Star Magnolia** white name - white flowers with yellow centers $12

☐ **Sweet Scented Gladiolus** white name - white flowers with purple centers $18

☐ **Sweet William** red name - red flowers with white centers and white flowers with red centers $12

☐ **Sunflower** gold name - gold flowers with black centers and highlights $14

☐ **Sunflower** – yellow name – yellow flowers with black centers and highlights $14

☐ **Trailing Arbutus** green name - pink flowers with dark green leaves $30

☐ **Tea** "tea" in green, "tea seed" in brown, and "tea leaves" in white - three different views of the tea plant RARE $100+

☐ **Tea** (not pictured) "tea" in green at bottom, "tea seed" in brown near middle, "tea flower" in white near top $100+

☐ **Trumpet Vine** red name near middle - red flowers with olive green centers and bases $30

☐ **Trailing Arbutus** pink name near middle - pink flowers with light green leaves $30

☐ **Trumpet Vine** red name near middle - red flowers with gold centers and gold bases $30

☐ **Trumpet Vine** maroon name - maroon flowers with gold centers and gold highlights $30

☐ **Tulip** red name near middle - entirely red flowers $8

☐ **Tulip** red name in slightly smaller script - red flowers with clear lines in petals and black centers $8

☐ **Tulip** red name in slightly larger script - red flowers with black centers $8

☐ **Tulip** dark pink name - dark pink flowers with black centers $8

☐ **Tulip** white name - white flowers with red tips $18

☐ **Tulip** white name - white flowers with black centers $35

☐ **Tulip** yellow name - yellow flowers with black centers and lighter green leaves $20

☐ **Tulip** yellow name - yellow flowers with black centers and darker green leaves $20

☐ **Tulip** yellow name - yellow flowers with red tips $18

☐ **Tulip** purple name - purple flowers with yellow centers $35

☐ **Tulips** red name near middle - entirely red flowers $8

☐ **Tulips** red flowers with deeper red bases $8

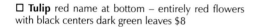

☐ **Tulips** red name - red flowers with black centers $8

☐ **Tulip** red name at bottom – entirely red flowers with black centers dark green leaves $8

☐ **Tulip** red name with dot at bottom – entirely red flowers with black centers and dark green leaves $8

☐ **Tulip** red name near middle – red flowers with dark red highlights and red stems medium green leaves $8

☐ **Tulip** white name with dot – white flowers with red tips dark green leaves $18

☐ **Tulips** yellow name - yellow flowers with black centers $20

☐ **Tulips** red name with dot – red flower with black centers $8

☐ **Tulips** small red name in middle – red flowers with dark red highlights medium green leaves $8

☐ **Tulips** deep yellow name – deep yellow flowers with black centers $18

☐ **Tulips** pale yellow name – pale yellow flowers with black centers $18

☐ **Viola** blue name - blue flowers with gold centers $25

☐ **Variegated Rose** red name - red and white flowers with medium green leaves $12

☐ **Violet** yellow name - yellow flowers with white centers $25

☐ **Variegated Rose** red name - red and white flowers with leaves that change from white to olive green $12

☐ **Variegated Rose** white name at bottom – all red flowers with a few white edges with one olive green leaf that is lighter at the bottom that top $12

☐ **Variegated Rose** white name at bottom – red flowers with a few olive and white edges, one olive green leaf that is a solid, even color $12

☐ **Violet** blue name - blue flowers with white centers $20

☐ **Violet** cream-colored name at top - purple flowers with cream-colored centers and lighter green leaves $20

☐ **Violet** purple name - purple flowers with cream-colored centers and darker green leaves $20

☐ **Violet** white name at top - yellow flowers with white centers $25

☐ **Violet** white name - white flowers with yellow centers $18

☐ **Violet** yellow name at top - white flowers with yellow centers $18

☐ **Violet** purple name - purple flowers with yellow centers in two bunches $30

☐ **Violet** blue name - blue flowers with yellow centers in two bunches $30

☐ **Violet** blue name – blue flowers with no other coloration on tumbler $30

☐ **Wake-Robin or Trillium** blue name - blue flowers with white centers and tips $14

☐ **Water Lily** green name - blue flowers with orange-gold centers $20

☐ **Wild Rose** pink name - pink flowers with yellow centers $20

☐ **Wild Rose** pink name near bottom on angle – e is written as backwards 3 – pink flowers with pale yellow centers $20

☐ **Wild Rose** pink name at very bottom – pink flowers with pale yellow centers $20

☐ **Windflower** blue name near center - small blue flowers with yellow centers $18

☐ **Windflower** pink name – large pink flowers with olive green centers and green lines on top of bud in back $18

☐ **Windflower** pink name – large pink flowers with yellow centers $18

☐ **Zinnia** orange name near middle - orange bushy flowers with darker orange separating each petal $14

Chapter 3
Iced Tea Size

There are 16 iced tea size peanut butter glasses in 14 different flowers. The tallest of the three sizes, they probably were never filled with peanut butter. I suspect they were produced to accompany the standard size peanut butter glasses, and since they were purchased less were produced.

Iced tea sized peanut butter glasses are the most difficult to locate. Due to their scarcity and high price many collectors do not purchase this size.

☐ **Amaryllis** red name - red flowers with white centers $40

☐ **California Poppy** yellow name - yellow flowers with green or yellow centers $30

☐ **Columbine** red name - red flowers with white centers $35

☐ **Columbine** blue name - blue flowers with white centers $30

☐ **Daffodil** yellow name - yellow flowers with red-orange centers $45

☐ **Columbine** red name - red flowers with gold centers $30

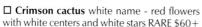

☐ **Crimson cactus** white name - red flowers with white centers and white stars RARE $60+

☐ **Dogwood** green name - pink flowers on the bottom and white flowers on the top with green circles in centers $100+

☐ **Primrose** red name - red flowers with yellow center $40

☐ **Michaelmas Daisy** purple name - purple flowers with gold centers $40

☐ **Morning Glory** blue name - blue flowers with white centers and lines coming from centers $45

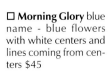

☐ **Rose** mustard name - blue flowers with mustard centers $45

☐ **Sweet Scented Gladiolus** white name - white flowers with purple centers $40

☐ **Tulips** red name - red flowers with black centers $40

☐ **Shasta Daisy** white name - white flowers with yellow centers $45

☐ **Viola** blue name - blue flowers with gold centers $45

Juice Size

Original boxe[s]
cartons with di[v...]
of each tumb[...]
tumblers [...]
along.

There are 42 different flowered glasses in 26 different nar[...] floral names are located either at the top in large letters or [...] script. The wordless Santa Claus tumbler is the most elusive [...] expensive.

Shown are four juice size tumblers that greatly resemb[...] They do have names near the bottom and graphics very similar to peanut butter glasses. Two key differences are, the fact that there are no stems, and the mold of the tumbler is done so that these have a rounded bottom. I have included these as, perhaps, they are peanut butter glasses and one of you readers can verify this. Regardless, they are lovely and perhaps collectible even if found not to be actual peanut butter glasses. Shown are a gold Dahlia, a blue Iris, a red Oriental-Poppy, and white Shasta Daisy.

The first half of this chapter is an alphabetical arrangement of the juice tumblers with the name at the top. This is followed by an alphabetical arrangement of juice tumblers with the name at the bottom.

of juice glasses continue to be found. These are plain white flip-top
...ders to hold eight tumblers. The arrangement we had consisted of two
...er: Pansy, Rose, Tulips, and Iris. As no lids have been found to fit the juice
...ne needs to assume they never really held peanut butter, but were a go-

☐ **Asters** blue name - dark blue bushy flowers with small amounts of light blue $45

☐ **Carnation** red name - red flowers with darker red highlights $35

☐ **Daisy** black name - yellow flowers with black centers and black lines mainly in top half of blossoms $40

☐ **Dogwood** yellow name - white flowers with yellow dots in centers $40

☐ **Iris** yellow name - gray flowers with yellow highlights $45

☐ **Iris** blue name - blue flowers with darker blue highlights $40

☐ **Morning Glory** white name - blue flowers with white centers and highlights $45

☐ **Pansy** black name - yellow and black flowers $30

☐ **Poppy** black name - red flowers with black centers and several lines coming out from centers $35

☐ **Rose** red name - red flowers with darker red highlights on each petal $35

☐ **Tulips** red name - red flowers with darker red highlights $30

Juice with names at bottom.

☐ **Asters** blue name - light blue bushy flowers having each petal outlined in dark blue also with a dark blue line in the center of each petal $45

☐ **Amaryllis** red name - red flowers with white centers $45

☐ **Azalea** red name - red flowers with black centers and highlights $45

☐ **Clematis** burgundy name – burgundy flowers with yellow centers and yellow curlicues $50

☐ **Carnation** red name – red flowers with deep red highlights $35

☐ **Columbine** blue name - blue flowers with white centers $40

☐ **Daffodils** yellow name - entirely yellow flowers $45

☐ **Christmas Rose** white name - white flowers with gold centers $45

☐ **Chrysanthemum** red name - red flowers with pale yellow centers $45

☐ **Daisy** yellow name on angle near middle – yellow flowers with black highlights, black centers $50

☐ **Dogwood** pink name - pink flowers with gold dots in centers $35

☐ **Dogwood** white name - white flowers with gold dots in centers $35

☐ **Pansy** yellow name – yellow flowers with really dark brown centers $35

☐ **Holly** red name - berries are completely red on one branch of leaves wrapped diagonally around glass $45

☐ **Iris** blue name - blue flowers with darker blue highlights $40

☐ **Iris** white name - gray flowers with yellow highlights $50

☐ **Pine** brown name - branches are full of needles and smaller pine cones $45

☐ **Michaelmas Daisy** blue name - blue flowers with gold centers and very narrow unpainted lines through centers of petals $40

☐ **Orchid** white name - gray flowers with yellow highlights $45

☐ **Pine** reddish brown name – branches have few needles with larger reddish brown pine cones, white lines of a snow scene encircle top of glass $50

☐ **Poppy** red name – red flower with black highlights $35

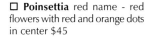

☐ **Pine** brown name - branches have few needles with larger pine cones, white lines of a snow scene encircle top of glass $45

☐ **Poinsettia** red name - red flowers with red and orange dots in center $45

☐ **Snowberry** white name - white berries with dark green leaves $45

☐ **Poinsettia** white name - white flowers with yellow centers $45

☐ **Sweet-Scented Gladiolus** white name - white flowers with purple centers $35

☐ **Violet** purple name - purple flowers with cream-colored centers $45

☐ **Tulips** yellow name - yellow flowers with black centers $40

☐ **Tulips** red name - red flowers with black centers $35

☐ **Santa** no writing RARE $100+

☐ **Tulips** red name on angle near middle – red flowers with dark red highlights $40

Chapter 5

Birds

There are 29 different glasses with 24 different birds. The names are written in a variety of sizes and styles and are found just about anywhere on the tumblers. Note that not all tumblers having bird designs are peanut butter glasses, although some sellers may tag them as if they are. The most common design of these look-alike glasses tapers in at the base, but peanut butter glasses are straight down.

Birds are not as popular as the flowered peanut butter glasses although songbirds are catching the interest of more collectors. They are not easily found which makes building a collection a bit of a challenge. One can expect to pay about $20-30 per songbird tumbler. Wild fowl such as ducks and pheasants sell for about $10 each.

☐ **Baltimore Oriole** $20-30   ☐ **Bluebird** $20-30

☐ **Blue Jay** $20-30

☐ **Bobolink** $20-30

☐ **Blue Jay** $20-30

☐ **cactus wren** $20-30

☐ **Cardinal** $20-30

☐ **Downy Woodpecker** $20-30

☐ **Duck** $10

☐ **Duck** $10

☐ **Gold Finch** $20-30   ☐ **Lazuli Bunting** $20-30

☐ **Killdeer** $20-30   ☐ **Meadowlark** $20-30

☐ **Meadowlark** $20-30

☐ **Mountain Bluebird** $20-30

☐ **Pheasant** $10

☐ **Meadowlark** $20-30

114

☐ **Quail** $10

☐ **Scarlet Tanager** $20-30

☐ **Western tanager** $20-30

☐ **Red Winged Blackbird** $20-30

☐ **Redstart** $20-30

☐ **Robin** $20-30

☐ **White Winged Crossbill** $20-30

☐ **Wild Geese** $10

☐ **Wood Thrush** $20-30

☐ **Wild Turkey** $10

☐ **Yellow Warbler** $20-30

Chapter 6

Dogs

I am delighted to have many more dog tumblers for presentation in this edition. These are not easily found and sell for about $35 each. Dog enthusiasts may be willing to pay considerably more for a particular tumbler if it features a breed of choice. We would love to find a West Highland White Terrier in honor of our Moxie.

As explained in the Introduction, it is believed that dog tumblers with a white name at the top in script contained Sweet Clover Homogenized Peanut Butter packed by Ehrhart Conrad Company, Inc., Hanover, Pennsylvania.

We found this juice bottle and felt it was worth sharing, as the six dogs are definitely the same graphics as those on dog peanut butter glasses. The names of the dogs encircle the bottom in a green band: Irish Setter, German Shepard, Dachshund, Springer Spaniel, Bassett Hound, French Poodle. It measures 6.5" in height and 3.75" in diameter.

☐ **Bassett Hound** $35

☐ **Beagle** $35

☐ **Boston Terrier** $35

☐ **Boston Terrier** $35

☐ **Boston Terrier** $35 (note: Wire-hair Terrier on other side)

☐ **Boxer** $35

☐ **Boxer** $35

☐ **Boxer** $35

□ Cocker Spaniel $35

□ Cocker Spaniel $35

□ Cocker
Spaniel $35

□ Collie $35

□ Dachshund $35

□ Dalmatian $35

☐ **Dalmatian** $35

☐ **Dalmatian $35** (note: Boxer on other side)

☐ **Doberman Pinscher** $35

☐ **English Setter** $35

☐ **German Shepherd** $35

☐ **German Shepherd** $35 (note: Collie on other side)

- ☐ **Great Dane** $35
- ☐ **Irish Setter** $35
- ☐ **Pekingese** $35
- ☐ **Pointer** $35

☐ **Poodle** $35

☐ **Poodle** $35

☐ **St. Bernard** $35

☐ **Scottish Terrier** $35

☐ **Smooth Hair Fox Terrier** $35

☐ **Springer Spaniel** $35 (note: no design on back)

☐ **Wire Haired Terrier** $35 (note: no design on back)

□ **Wire-haired Terrier** $35

□ **English Setter** $35 (note: Springer Spaniel on other side)

Racing Greyhound glasses are also peanut butter glasses. These were made with all the dogs on a tumbler having the same number. Shown are three (black), six (yellow), and eight (green); missing are one, two, four, five, and seven. I do not know how high the numbers continue, but I suspect eight is the highest. Note that on one side of the tumbler there is one greyhound, and on the other side there are two. These are worth about $25 each.

□ One

□ Two

□ Threee

□ Four

□ Five

□ Six

□ Seven

□ Eight

Chapter 7

Others

A variety of tumblers seem to be peanut butter glasses. The more people exchange memories, the more verification we have. All of the following ARE peanut butter glasses, with one question, the orange.

The orange tumbler seems to be right. That is, the size and weight of the glass are correct. We have only seen this one and suspect that more fruit may be "out there" somewhere. There is no writing on this tumbler, just the fruit, leaves, and stem.

Christmas

The six Christmas tumblers are extremely popular, even among non-collectors as they offer a seasonal appeal. The most common design is "Santa standing with toys at feet" and is actually found in two shades of red: a deeper burgundy red and cherry red that are equal in value. The cherry red tumbler features a ball to the right of the train car. The remainder of styles are difficult to find. Many overlook the candle but die-hard peanut butter glass collectors know that it is a rarity.

It is important to note that a plethora of look-alikes are available. The graphics that are found on some of these Christmas tumblers are found on other glassware as well. Shown are four of the many variations. These are not peanut butter glasses.

☐ Candle $40

☐ St. Nick with finger to lips $40

☐ Santa in green chimney $40

☐ St. Nick heads $50

☐ Santa standing with toys at feet, cherry red (shown) $20

☐ Santa standing with toys at feet, burgundy (not shown) $20

□ **St. Nick outside Post Office** $40

Nameless Florals

Six new tumblers are added to this often overlooked category: Daffodil, Pansy, Scabiosa, Sweet William, and two Tulips. Few collectors, in fact only the most serious collectors, show interest in these tumblers that were produced without names. These are not common, but due to an overall limited interest in them the prices remain suppressed. Again, supply and demand dictates value. The supply of nameless florals is low, but so is the demand.

We begin with a comparison. First is shown a Magnolia with the name (left) and one without (right). Most dealers will find the Magnolia with the name much easier to sell although it is a lot more common than its nameless counterpart. Expect to pay about $10-20 for any of these nameless floral tumblers.

☐ **Pine** - dark

☐ **Cosmos** - white and yellow

☐ **Daffodil** white flowers with gold centers – light green leaves that have gold tips & stems end in gold

☐ **Pine** - light

☐ **Holly Leaves**

☐ **Pansy (not pictured)** yellow flower with brown highlights

127

☐ **Scabiosa** - white

☐ **Scabiosa** - red

☐ **Scabiosa** blue flowers with white highlights

☐ **Sweet William** (not shown) red and white flowers

☐ **Tulips** three red blossoms with dark green leaves

☐ **Tulips** one red blossom and one red bud with dark green leaves

Dogs

Here is the nameless dog tumbler. As with the nameless florals the general lack of interest in an unlabeled glass keeps the value down.

☐ **Boxer** $20

These unnamed tumblers have been verified to be peanut butter glasses. Although the floral presentation is different from the others in the book, they are a lovely tumbler that serious collectors will not overlook. Expect to pay around $20 per tumbler.

☐ **Blue**

☐ **Pink**

☐ **White**

☐ **Yellow**

Davy Crockett

Found was an iced tea sized Davy Crockett tumbler that was 6-1/8" tall with a 3" diameter. The graphic was in white and the writing at the bottom, "Davy Crockett Frontier Hero 1786-1836" in pink. One can assume there are additional variations in this size. As this is a more difficult to find size, the value is $40. Other Davy Crockett peanut butter glasses are worth $25 each. Found but not pictured is a Davy Crockett Indian Fighter – Hero of Alamo with a white Alamo that is usually pictured in yellow.

Deer

New additions to the book include these deer tumblers: Virginia Deer and Prong-Horn Antelope. One would suspect that there are more in this series. Expect to pay $20 each.

☐ Virginia Deer

☐ Prong-Horn Deer

Butterfly and Fish

Since photographing the Java Birdwing butterfly glass I have not seen this tumbler again, or any additional butterfly glasses making this among the most rare of all peanut butter glasses. Expect to pay $100 or more if you are lucky enough to find one.

The fish tumblers are two-sided. That is, there is one fish shown and named on one side and another one on the opposite side. Shown are two new fish peanut butter glasses. Fish glasses are valued at $75 each.

☐ **Java Birdwing** $100

☐ **Northern Pike/Small Mouth Bass** names in pink $75

☐ **Crappie/Yellow Perch** names in teal $75

☐ **Sunfish/Muskellunge** names in green and pink $75

☐ **Walleye Pike/ Rainbow Trout** names in yellow $75

132

Transportation Series

Amour Peanut Butter was available in a series of primarily black and white tumblers that depicted various modes of transportation. Shown are:

- ☐ The Automobile
- ☐ The Covered Wagon
- ☐ The High Wheel Bicycle
- ☐ The Locomotive
- ☐ The River Steamboat
- ☐ The Stage Coach
- ☐ The Tandem Bike

These are 5" tall and have a 2.75" diameter. As these are not particularly popular the values remain at $10 each. Not shown is the Sleigh and several others.

Wizard of Oz

Shown are three versions of the same graphic: "The Wizard of Oz Dorothy." There are minute measurement differences in these Swift Peanut Butter glasses, but distinct differences in the tumblers themselves. One tumbler comes straight down, one has a corrugated base, and one has four bands of waves at the very bottom. The straight tumbler is 4-7/8" tall with a 2.75" diameter. The corrugated base is 5" tall with a 2-7/16" diameter. The wavy-based tumbler is 4-15/16" tall with a 2-5/8" diameter. The value of the three designs is the same, $25 each, and all three can be found with the following graphics:

☐ Dorothy (shown)
☐ Glinda
☐ Lion
☐ Scarecrow
☐ Toto
☐ Wizard
☐ Woodsman

Chapter 8

REPRODUCTIONS

Unfortunately whenever something gets popular it seems as though reproductions follow. There are a variety of tumblers that appear to be peanut butter glasses. The sizes and shapes of peanut butter glasses are fairly standard and have been meticulously provided in the introduction. If the tumbler in question seems slightly different it may not be a peanut butter glass. Glassware in question may be lighter weight, tapered at the bottom or found with a bead of glass at the rim. Some dealers are using the identifying term "Peanut Butter Glass" on any tumbler that has a flower motif so shop with care. I am not convinced that all look-alikes are actually reproductions, that is newly made specifically as copycat items, but may be from the same period of time as actual peanut butter glasses.

While in Canada I found these three Hyacinth tumblers. The graphics are certainly reminiscent of peanut butter glasses, but the dimensions of these tumblers are a bit different than those provided earlier in the book. Based on the glass itself I would venture to say these are not peanut butter glasses. However, I am not 100% certain.

There is one reproduction that must be noted, as this is a brand new piece that I have seen priced as if old: Cream Dove Brand Peanut Butter Salad Dressing Cream Dove Mfg., Co., Inc. Binghamton, N.Y. measuring cup. The wording is in capitals on a one-cup measure. I have pictured it in green, but it is found in pink as well. The glass is of poor quality with bubbles and a bit of cloudiness, and will feel oily to the touch. Remember, this is brand new!